Little People, BIG DREAMS
HARRIET TUBMAN

Written by
Mª Isabel Sánchez Vegara

Illustrated by
Pili Aguado

Lincoln
Children's Books

Minty was a little girl who was born into slavery in Maryland. She was owned by white masters and forced to work for them from dawn to dusk. At night, while her family slept, she wished to be free...

But freedom was a faraway dream for Minty—and many other African Americans living in the South. Slave owners were allowed to sell people as if they were property.

And one day, Minty's owners sold three of her sisters. Minty and her parents wondered if they would ever see them again.

Every other day, Minty was beaten by her masters. But she was always ready to stand up for herself and others.

One morning, while protecting a slave who was trying to escape his overseer, she was hit on the head.

For Minty, that blow was a sign that marked
her destiny: she was now more determined
than ever to take her people to the Northern
states, where slavery no longer existed.

So one night, she said goodbye to her family and started a long journey north, to Philadelphia, guided by the North Star. Minty changed her name to Harriet so she couldn't be traced.

When Harriet finally reached Philadelphia, she joined the Underground Railroad—a secret network of safe houses and

people who were against slavery. They helped enslaved men and women reach safety in the free states and Canada.

Thanks to them, Harriet
soon traveled to the South again.
She went back for her brothers and sisters,
and as many slaves as needed her help.

For 11 years, Harriet repeated the same trip again and again, guiding hundreds of people to the safety of the Northern states. She called them her "passengers," and she never lost a single one.

After years of problems between the Northern and Southern states, a civil war broke out. Harriet signed up to help as a cook. But she soon became a nurse, and even a spy, too!

On a mission to rescue seven hundred slaves, Harriet led three steamboats along rivers full of explosives. She became a hero, and everybody called her "Moses," after the Bible story.

Eventually, the war came to an end, and there was a great celebration. Slavery was finally over, and millions of people were free for the first time in their lives.

But Harriet's work was not finished. Unequal rules for African Americans carried on long after slavery was over. She took to the stage to demand her rights.

Because little Harriet knew that you have to use all of your strength to stand up for yourself so that you can stand up for others, too.

HARRIET TUBMAN

(Born 1822 • Died 1913)

c. 1868

c. 1875

Araminta "Minty" Ross was born into slavery on a plantation in Maryland. A slave is someone who is owned by another person and is forced to work for them without being paid. Slavery was legal in America when Minty was born. The first slave in Minty's family was her grandmother who was taken from her home in Africa and brought to America on a ship. She was enslaved by white owners. Minty's family, along with many others, worked on plantations—places where crops were grown. Minty was forced to work from the age of five. But she had a fighting spirit and always stood up for herself and others. One day, a man hit her on the head while she was trying to help a runaway slave. The injury was

c. 1885   2009

so bad that she was in pain for the rest of her life. In 1849, Minty
made a plan to escape. She changed her name to Harriet Tubman
and made a dangerous journey north to the states where slavery no
longer existed. Once she was free, she went back for others. The
skills she picked up on these missions helped her during the Civil
War. She led an operation to free hundreds of slaves, crippling the
plantation where they worked. In her later years, Harriet spoke up
about women's rights and helped the people she had freed to start
new lives, as laws were still unequal for African Americans. Harriet
sacrificed so much throughout her life to help others. She is a symbol
of strength, hope, and bravery for many people around the world.

Want to find out more about **Harriet Tubman?**
Read one of these great books:

Minty: A Story of Young Harriet Tubman by Alan Schroeder and Jerry Pinkney
Who Was Harriet Tubman? by Yona Zeldis McDonough and Nancy Harrison
I Am Harriet Tubman by Brad Meltzer and Christopher Eliopoulos

If you're in Maryland, you could even visit the Harriet Tubman Underground
Railroad State Park to learn more about her life.

Brimming with creative inspiration, how-to projects, and useful information to enrich your everyday life, Quarto Knows is a favorite destination for those pursuing their interests and passions. Visit our site and dig deeper with our books into your area of interest: Quarto Creates, Quarto Cooks, Quarto Homes, Quarto Lives, Quarto Drives, Quarto Explores, Quarto Gifts, or Quarto Kids.

Text © 2018 Mª Isabel Sánchez Vegara. Illustrations © 2018 Pili Aguado.

First published in the UK in 2018 by Lincoln Children's Books, an imprint of The Quarto Group.
400 First Avenue North, Suite 400, Minneapolis, MN 55401, USA.
T (612) 344-8100 F (612) 344-8692 **www.QuartoKnows.com**
First published in Spain in 2018 under the title Pequeña & Grande Harriet Tubman
by Alba Editorial, s.l.u., Baixada de Sant Miquel, 1, 08002 Barcelona
www.albaeditorial.es

A catalog record for this book is available from the British Library.
ISBN 978-1-78603-227-0

The illustrations were created with ink, markers, and digital techniques. Set in Futura BT

Published by Rachel Williams • Designed by Karissa Santos
Edited by Katy Flint • Production by Jenny Cundill

Manufactured in Guangdong, China CC072018

9 8 7 6 5 4 3 2

Photographic acknowledgments (pages 28–29, from left to right) 1. Harriet Tubman, 1868–1869 from the Collection of the Smithsonian National Museum of African American History and Culture shared with the Library of Congress. 2. Harriet Tubman, 1860–1875 © copyright Alpha Historica / Alamy Stock Photo. 3. Harriet Tubman, 1885 © copyright GL Archive / Alamy Stock Photo. 4. Harriet Tubman Monument in Boston Massachusetts, 2009 © copyright Anthony Pleva / Alamy Stock Photo.

Also in the *Little People,* **BIG DREAMS** series:

FRIDA KAHLO

ISBN: 978-1-84780-783-0

Meet Frida Kahlo, one of the best artists of the twentieth century.

COCO CHANEL

ISBN: 978-1-84780-784-7

Discover the life of Coco Chanel, the famous fashion designer.

MAYA ANGELOU

ISBN: 978-1-84780-889-9

Read about Maya Angelou—one of the world's most loved writers.

AMELIA EARHART

ISBN: 978-1-84780-888-2

Learn about Amelia Earhart—the first female to fly solo over the Atlantic.

AGATHA CHRISTIE

ISBN: 978-1-78603-220-1

Meet the queen of the imaginative mystery—Agatha Christie.

MARIE CURIE

ISBN: 978-1-84780-962-9

Be introduced to Marie Curie, the Nobel Prize–winning scientist.

ROSA PARKS

ISBN: 978-1-78603-018-4

Discover the life of Rosa Parks, the first lady of the civil rights movement.

AUDREY HEPBURN

ISBN: 978-1-78603-053-5

Learn about the iconic actress and humanitarian—Audrey Hepburn.

EMMELINE PANKHURST

ISBN: 978-1-78603-019-1

Meet Emmeline Pankhurst, the suffragette who helped women get the vote.

ELLA FITZGERALD

ISBN: 978-1-78603-087-0

Meet Ella Fitzgerald, the pioneering jazz singer and musician.

ADA LOVELACE

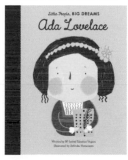

ISBN: 978-1-78603-076-4

Read all about Ada Lovelace, the first computer programmer.

GEORGIA O'KEEFFE

ISBN: 978-1-78603-122-8

Discover the life of Georgia O'Keeffe, the famous American painter.

JANE AUSTEN

ISBN: 978-1-78603-120-4

Learn about Jane Austen, the beloved English writer.